# The Really Wild Life of Birds of Prey™

# BALD EAGLES

## DOUG WECHSLER
### THE ACADEMY OF NATURAL SCIENCES

The Rosen Publishing Group's
PowerKids Press™
New York

For Neil, 3, who shares my appreciation of eagles.

About the Author
*Wildlife biologist, ornithologist, and photographer Doug Wechsler has studied birds, snakes, frogs, and other wildlife around the world. Doug Wechsler works at The Academy of Natural Sciences of Philadelphia, a natural history museum. As part of his job, he travels to rain forests and remote parts of the world to take pictures of birds. He has taken part in expeditions to Ecuador, the Philippines, Borneo, Cuba, Cameroon, and many other countries.*

Published in 2001 by The Rosen Publishing Group, Inc.
29 East 21st Street, New York, NY 10010

First Edition

Book Design: Michael de Guzman

Photo Credits: p. 4 © A. & S. Carey/VIREO; p. 6 © R. Curtis/VIREO; p. 7 © A. & E. Morris/VIREO; p. 8 © John Cancalosi/VIREO; p. 11 © A. & S. Carey/VIREO; p. 12 © A. Morris/VIREO; p.15 © A. Carey/VIREO; p.16 © Fred K. Truslow/VIREO; p. 19 © A. & S. Carey/VIREO; p. 20 © A. Morris/VIREO; p. 22 © T. Vezo/VIREO. All photographs from VIREO (Visual Resources for Ornithology), The Academy of Natural Sciences' worldwide collection of bird photographs.

Wechsler, Doug.
        Bald Eagles / by Doug Wechsler.
            p. cm — (The really wild life of birds of prey)
    Summary: Introduces bald eagles, the symbol of the United States, describing their physical characteristics, habits, and life cycle.
        ISBN 0-8239-5595-8 (lib. bdg. : alk. paper)
        1. Bald eagle—Juvenile literature. [1. Bald eagle. 2. Eagles.] I. Series.
QL696.F32 W43 2000
598.9'43—dc21

                                                                    99-044809
                                                                        CIP

Manufactured in the United States of America

# CONTENTS

1  What Is a Bald Eagle?                          5

2  At Home on the Shore                           6

3  Rotten Fish, Favorite Dish                     9

4  If You Can't Get It Rotten, Eat It Fresh!     10

5  The Rest of the Menu                          13

6  A Nest As Heavy As Your Car                   14

7  An Eaglet Is Born                             17

8  Going Bald                                    18

9  An All-American Bird                          21

10 The Bald Eagle Comeback                       22

   Glossary                                      23

   Index                                         24

   Web Sites                                     24

**DOUG SAYS**

AN EAGLE ON THE MOVE FLIES AT ABOUT 40 MILES (64 KILOMETERS) PER HOUR.

# WHAT IS A BALD EAGLE?

A big, brown, large-winged bird **soars** above. From its white head and white tail you know right away it is an adult bald eagle. Its eyes and beak are bright yellow. The wings look like they might be longer than your bed, maybe 8 feet (2 meters) from tip to tip. Though the eagle has huge wings, it is not very heavy. It weighs only about 10 pounds (4 kilograms), the same as a pet cat.

Eagles are part of a group of birds called **raptors**. Raptors are also called birds of **prey** because they eat other animals. Raptors have powerful feet with sharp claws. These claws are used for grabbing prey.

*Bald eagles and other raptors have a hooked beak for tearing apart their prey.*

Bald eagles like to be near water where they can find fish. They live near rivers, lakes, and saltwater coasts. Eagles like a home with a view where they can watch over their land. They perch in high places like treetops, cliffs, or rock piles. Eagles have very good eyesight. This helps them see their food at a great distance. With their eagle eyes, they can spot a rabbit over a mile (2 kilometers) away.

*Bald eagles like to live near rivers, lakes, and seacoasts. More Bald eagles can be found in Alaska than in any other place in the world.*

ALASKA

# ROTTEN FISH, FAVORITE DISH

An eagle likes nothing better than a meal of **carrion**. Carrion is dead animal flesh. An eagle's favorite carrion is fish. Maybe this is because fish carrion is easy to find near the water. Also, it takes a lot less work to catch a dead fish than a live one. Like other animals, eagles are lazy when they can be.

The largest groups of eagles are found where salmon **spawn** and die. Each November, over 3,000 eagles feed along the Chilkat River in Alaska. Together they feast on dead salmon. This is the biggest gathering of bald eagles in the world.

*A bald eagle gets ready to munch on a rotting salmon.*

# IF YOU CAN'T GET IT ROTTEN, EAT IT FRESH!

If an eagle cannot find carrion, it goes fishing. First the eagle waits on a good lookout perch. When it spots a fish near the surface of the water, the eagle takes off. As the eagle is flying toward the fish, its legs reach forward. The powerful **talons** snatch the fish. Without missing a **wingbeat**, the eagle flies away with its dinner. Then, the eagle settles on a safe perch to begin eating.

As strange as it sounds, eagles also hunt fish in the air. They steal fish from other birds such as ospreys and other eagles that are flying by. Bald eagles will hunt on foot, too. They wade into rivers full of fish and grab their prey with their talons.

*A bald eagle barely gets wet as it snatches a fish from the water.*

# THE REST OF THE MENU

After fish, birds are a bald eagle's next favorite food. Bald eagles prey on ducks, geese, and other birds that live near water. An eagle will fly over a large **flock** of birds looking for one bird that is easy to catch. Sometimes a pair of eagles will hunt ducks together. As the first eagle attacks, the duck dives under water. When the duck comes up, the other eagle is ready to make the catch.

Some eagles spend the winter away from water. They go to the warmer, dry valleys of the western United States. There are no fish or **waterfowl** in these areas, so these eagles spend the colder months munching on jackrabbits and dead cows.

*An adult eagle has captured an American coot, a common bird found near shallow lakes and marshes.*

13

# A NEST AS HEAVY AS YOUR CAR

A pair of bald eagles usually builds its nest in a very sturdy tree. The nest is built to last many years. The birds add sticks to the nest every year, so the nest gets very heavy. To build these nests, eagles carry many fat sticks into the tree. They place grass and moss on top of the sticks. This makes a soft platform on which the female can lay her eggs. The heaviest bald eagle nest ever found weighed 2 tons (tonnes). That is probably heavier than your family's car. The nest was 9 1/2 feet (3 meters) across and 20 feet (6 meters) deep. Most nests are about 5 feet (2 meters) wide and 3 feet (1 meter) deep.

*Bald eagles start to nest very early in spring, sometimes before the snow melts.*

# AN EAGLET IS BORN

A female bald eagle can lay up to three eggs. The parents take turns **incubating** the eggs for 35 days. Afterward, the chicks break out of the eggs. The eaglets are covered with fuzzy **down**. The parents tear off bits of fish they catch to feed the newborns. The eaglets eat every three hours.

In the first week, the eaglets grow to four times their **birth weight**. In two weeks time, they may be 10 times heavier than they were at birth. Stiff feathers soon replace the down. Then the eaglets flap their wings for exercise. Next, they sail from one side of the nest to the other. After two and a half months, they are ready to fly from the nest.

*A bald eagle feeds its 13-day-old chick. The chick's down will be replaced by stiff feathers within two months.*

# GOING BALD

The first year is the toughest for a young eagle. It has to learn certain skills or it will die. It must learn how to hunt and fish. It must learn how to soar. It must even learn to be lazy, so that it does not waste energy. During its first year, an eagle is the color of dark chocolate. If it makes it past the first year, it grows white feathers on its breast and belly. In the fourth year, a young eagle trades its white feathers for brown ones. It starts to grow white feathers on its head and tail. After about five years, an eagle has a full white head and tail. The white head and tail show that it is an adult. The white head of the adult eagle makes the bird look bald. This is why it is called a bald eagle.

*A young eagle fishes. From the white feathers on the breast, we can guess it is about two or three years old.*

## DOUG SAYS

AN EAGLE'S FEATHERS WEIGH MORE THAN TWICE AS MUCH AS ITS BONES.

**DOUG SAYS**

THE BALD EAGLE WAS THE FIRST BIRD FEATURED ON A U.S. POSTAGE STAMP.

# AN ALL-AMERICAN BIRD

The bald eagle has been the national **symbol** of the United States since 1782. You can see this symbol in many places. Look on dollar bills, on the tops of flagpoles, and on the **seal** in front of the President when he speaks. Because of its strength and grace, the bald eagle has become a symbol of freedom and greatness. When the American **forefathers** chose the eagle, not everyone approved. Ben Franklin thought the eagle might be too lazy to be the national symbol. He suggested the turkey instead, but no one else agreed. Bald eagles are truly an American bird. They fly over every state but Hawaii and live only in North America.

*Is there an eagle in your pocket? Check the backs of your dollars and quarters.*

# THE BALD EAGLE COMEBACK

Bald eagles almost disappeared from the United States by 1970. **DDT**, a chemical used to kill insects, washed into our rivers and lakes and ended up in the bald eagles' food. When the eagles ate the fish, the DDT made their eggshells thin. The thin-shelled eggs were crushed by the parents when they tried to incubate the eggs.

In 1972, Congress banned DDT. With the help of scientists, bald eagles have made a big comeback. Now they are no longer an **endangered species**. We still must protect the sturdy trees where they make their homes. We must take care of the rivers and lakes where they find food. With our help, bald eagles will always be America's living symbol.

# GLOSSARY

**birth weight** (BERTH WAYT)  The weight of a baby animal when it is born.

**carrion** (KA-ree-un)  Dead, rotting flesh of animals.

**DDT** (D D T)  A kind of insecticide, or poison meant to kill insects.

**down** (DOWN)  A covering of soft, fluffy feathers.

**endangered species** (en-DAYN-jerd SPEE-sheez)  A species, or kind of animal, that will probably die out if we don't protect it or the place where it lives.

**flock** (FLOK)  A group of the same kind of animals, keeping, eating, or herding together.

**forefathers** (FOR-fa-thurz)  Early Americans.

**incubating** (IN-kyoo-bayt-ing)  Keeping eggs warm so they can hatch.

**prey** (PRAY)  To eat other animals for food.

**raptors** (RAP-terz)  Sharp-clawed birds that hunt other animals.

**seal** (SEEL)  A design used as an official mark.

**soars** (SORZ)  When a bird flies in the air without flapping its wings.

**spawn** (SPAWN)  To lay eggs in water.

**symbol** (SIM-bul)  Something that represents or stands for something else.

**talons** (TAL-uns)  Sharp, curved claws on a bird of prey.

**waterfowl** (WAT-er-fowl)  Ducks, geese, swans, and similar water birds.

**wingbeat** (WING-beet)  A stroke of the wing up and down when a bird is flying.

# INDEX

**B**
beak, 5

**C**
carrion, 9, 10
chicks, 17
claws, 5

**D**
DDT, 22

**E**
eyes, 5, 6

**F**
feathers, 17, 18
fish, 6, 9, 10, 13,
    17, 18, 22

**H**
head, 5, 18
hunt, 10, 13, 18

**N**
nest, 14, 17

**P**
prey, 5, 10, 13

**R**
raptors, 5

**T**
tail, 5, 18
talons, 10

**W**
wings, 5, 17

# WEB SITES

To learn more about bald eagles and raptors, check out these Web sites:

http://www.raptor.cvm.umn.edu/
http://www.acnatsci.org/vireo (Readers can order a raptor slide set.)
http://www.baldeagleinfo.com